This book is
dedicated to
my wife and children.

Thanks

— ■ ■ ■ —

All Scripture quotations, unless otherwise noted, are taken from the
Holy Bible: New International Version.®

Designed by: JrT | creative**DESIGNS**

Steven E. Richie is a licensed minister who preaches the Gospel of Jesus Christ and is currently pursuing a Master's Degree in Christian Education. Steven is married and the father of four children and a graduate of the University of Illinois Springfield (*formerly Sangamon State University*).

He may be contacted at:
sbwcsr@yahoo.com

Shoebox
Chicken

Seven Life Lessons
that Every Person Should Know

FOREWORD

Five years ago we added an additional 40,000 square feet to the existing 16,500 square feet building. It was a major project that required serious planning if the outcome was going to be a success. Of course there were change orders which were unforeseen things that caused us to readjust then move forward. But in order to avoid any mishaps that would completely stop the progress of the building the architect's blue print had to be followed to the lesson. The Christian walk is very similar to the construction of a major building. To avoid any unnecessary set backs or delays we must follow the practical principles of God.

Minister Steven Richie has taken the simplicity of God's word and put it into "Shoe Box Chicken." Someone once said, "Experience is the best teacher." It is within the pages of this book Minister Richie has taken his personal experiences to reveal God's spiritual truths. Each of us has experiences in life; some are good and some are not so pleasant. The design of "Shoe Box Chicken" causes the reader to immediately create a journal in which Minister Richie calls a faith file. As you create and reflect on your faith file it is through these seven life lessons you will discover that God takes ordinary people and does extra ordinary things.

Chapter one gives you the aroma of shoe box chicken. As you begin to bite into chapter two, I promise you that you will not stop until you are spiritually licking your fingers in chapter seven. In the words of Minister Richie, "It's good for you, good to you, and will sustain you for the journey."

I think this book should be added to every membership, discipleship and orientation class. No college student or military enlistee should leave home without it.

T. Ray McJunkins, *Senior Pastor*
Union Baptist Church
Springfield, IL

From me **to you...**

About five years ago, I was introduced to the phrase "faith file" by Nick, an old high school classmate. Nick had come back to town to see his oldest son play in a football game at our old high school. At that particular time I was at a low point in life. I had been having trouble on the job and was at home on administrative leave pending an internal investigation. Nick had heard about this and wanted to offer words of encouragement. He simply said "do you have faith?" My reply was an obvious and adamant— "Yes." Next, came "look into your faith file."

Nick went on to explain that a faith file is where we as believers are to file away all of our life's experiences the good and the perceived bad, recognizing that God alone brought us through those times. The faith file can be kept tucked in mental memories, on a legal pad, or laptop. It does not matter where you keep your faith file, just as long as you have one at your ready disposal. After leaving Nick, I went home and began to jot down major episodes that had occurred in my life the painful and the pleasing. Wouldn't you know it, Nick was right. I then opened the bible and read about one of my favorite bible heroes— David. It was right there in **I Samuel Chapter 17**. David was going to fight the giant Goliath. David's brothers ridiculed him for even attempting such a feat. King Saul even doubted him. David was not dissuaded he simply opened his mental faith file and replied, "I kept my father's sheep and there came a lion and a bear and took a lamb out of the flock. I went out after him and hit him and took the lamb out of his mouth. When the animal got up to harm me, I took him by the beard and hit him and killed him. Thy servant has killed both a lion and a bear. And this Philistine is going to be just like one of those animals since he has defied the armies of the living God." David continued, "the Lord that saved and delivered me out of the claws of the lion and the claws of the bear will deliver me out of the hand of this Philistine."

We all know how this episode in David's life ended— one stone, one throw, one dead Goliath.

So as you read Shoebox Chicken, it is my hope and desire that these episodes from my faith file will cause you to not only find strength from my journey, but to also cause you to create your own faith file.

What you need to remember is that a faith file is personal. The faith file is the diary of what has happened in your life: the gory details of each tragedy and the unexplainable joy of triumphs and successes.

Oh by the way, the investigation concluded, and like Joseph in the bible I can say "what others meant for evil God meant for my good, and I am in a good place." Back to work and prospering very well.

– Thank you Jesus.

The title **explained...**

My brothers and I are products of the late 50's and 60's. We are children of parents who left the state of Mississippi in search of a better life up north. We would routinely make the holiday journeys back to Mississippi to see our grandparents on the farm. The most common holiday travel times were July 4th (when it was hot as a big one); Labor Day weekend and often Thanksgiving. Although life was not as it was all cracked up to be in the good old north, it was still a lot better than life in the south. In the 60's, society was still not fully integrated. It was not uncommon to see crosses ablaze in the distance as we traversed the two lane roads headed south. These were cautious times, as blacks were not welcomed at every restaurant along the way. In preparing us for a long night of travel, our mother would prepare for our father, a meal fit for a king: vanilla wafers with cheddar cheese, apples, pound cake and of course— fried chicken. This was a time before zip lock bags and plastic containers, so improvisation was necessary. My mother, along with just about every black woman traveling south during this time, would line a shoe box with aluminum foil and place the piping hot chicken inside. Hence, the name— Shoebox Chicken. Shoebox Chicken —good for you, to you and would sustain you throughout the journey. In keeping with the theme of preparation for the journey, it is my hope that you will agree the lessons shared in this book will be good for you, to you and will sustain you throughout your life's journey.

Contents

Doubt and faith   **1**

Choosing your friends   **10**

It is not what you're called,
it's what you answer to   **15**

Don't give up!   **20**

Now and later   **25**

Guard your dreams   **32**

Go and possess the land   **36**

Doubt and **faith**

Faith is defined in the bible as being sure of what we hope for and certain of what we do not see. "Faith is the substance of things hoped for and the evidence of things not seen."

We all have a measure of faith but we really don't know what we have until our faith is tested. Faith is what remains when all else fails. Faith is what we have when we can't see our way out of our troubles. Faith is what we have when we need to talk to someone and no one answers our phone call. Faith answers the question "what will I do now?" Faith gives us hope when others have written us off. Faith is what we have when doors are slammed closed in our faces. Faith is what we have when our friends have turned their backs on us.

There is one thing that gets in the way of our faith: doubt— in either our selves or in God.

Recently my family and I gathered with other family members for a 4th of July celebration. My nephew Jerry graciously agreed to host this gathering of aunts, uncles, 1st and 2nd cousins and a few friends. You have to know Jerry. He is what we call "military organized." He leaves no stone unturned. He dots each "I" and crosses every "T." He took the appropriate steps to ensure that no one would have trouble finding his house. Everyone was to feel welcomed in his home. He did a MapQuest of the directions to his house, and emailed greetings and directions to all those traveling. We all printed the directions. There were others who just entered his address into the global positioning system (GPS).

Armed with directions and the assigned side dishes we each began our treks to Jerry's house. Whitney who had never been to Peoria, Illinois before set out following the directions. For those of you who have been to Peoria from Springfield you take 55 North to 155 North, 74 West to 474 West to exit 2. There is a nearly unbroken view of corn and soybean fields which blanket the landscape in the summertime.

Whitney followed the directions nearly all the way—exits 10, 9, 8, 7, 6, 5, 4, and 3. Then without warning, exit A to Moline and exit B to Peoria appear. Jerry's directions were very clear, "follow until you get to exit 2." Now mind you Whitney had never been to Peoria. Because she had never been and did not really know her way, up until now followed the directions explicitly without problem. Doubt pops up— 5, 4, 3, A and B this doesn't add up— she takes exit A and heads toward Moline— the wrong way. Sensing that something is amiss, Whitney calls Jerry. The author of the directions. The host of the gathering. The one who actually lives in Peoria. Jerry hears the uncertainty in her voice, "cousin Jerry I think I took the wrong exit." Jerry is able to locate her without leaving his house. What he says next is as profound a statement as anyone can tell a lost person. He simply tells her— "turn around." She makes a u-turn. Now heading in the right direction, she drives past exits A and B. Just beyond the bend in the road is exit 2. She takes the exit and makes it in time for the catfish and the next game of spades. Jerry greets her with a hug and reassurance.

Now it's my story. I had been to Jerry's house before and this is all familiar territory 10, 9, 8, 7, 6, 5, 4, 3, A and B exit 2. I got this. But guess what, doubt— begins to take over. Road construction has erased the familiarity of the land marks. Believe it or not I hesitated, even beads of sweat began to form on my brow. In my hesitation I almost took exit A to Moline. At the last moment, I remembered Jerry's directions. I began to talk to myself "come on Steve, get a grip." I recalled that I had previously followed the same directions the last time I visited and arrived without incident (faith file). I keep straight and just ahead around the bend is exit 2— all is well.

Robert is the GPS traveler. He follows the GPS which takes him through heavy road construction and a bevy of trooper check points. His journey is delayed, fraught with barricades and danger. He makes it to Jerry's house.

It is at the house, in the middle of a game of spades, surrounded by the aroma of fried catfish, baked beans, pineapple upside cake, and honey barbequed wings that we all begin to recount our journeys. Whitney and I confess that we had doubts— doubts in ourselves as well as Jerry's directions. Logic got in the way. Jerry pointed out that Whitney lacked complete trust or faith in him and his directions, although she had never been to his house. In the end, it was Jerry who helped her turn around and get back on the right road.

As for me, although I had prior experience with the directions Jerry had given me, I still doubted him. I almost gave up and headed in the wrong direction. All I had to do was journey just a little further. We talked about what got in my way. We narrowed it down to the obstacles which were not present the last time I visited him. As Robert began to deal another hand of spades, he boasted that he arrived at the right destination, without any hesitation at all. He had complete faith in his GPS. I played the big Joker and raked in the cards. Jerry took this point in the game to tell Robert that had he followed the directions given, he would have arrived without incident. Jerry's directions, would have brought Robert around the barricades, construction and police check points. Robert's journey then would have been quicker, and less frustrating.

There will be times in your life when doubt in either self or in your faith may cause you to miss the mark, and have you headed in the wrong direction. But just as with Whitney it is up to you to reach out to God: admit that you are headed in the wrong direction. God being the god of mercy and grace—allows u-turns. Because he is omnipresent he will meet you where you are and redirect your life. In my situation, the importance, of having a faith file and paying attention to the faith file really came to life. The faith file can be either mental or in written form and is used to chronicle the manifestation of the works of God in the life of the believer. When doubt arises, it is important for you to draw from the events in your personal faith file to get through episodes of doubt. Robert's episode unfortunately is an all too familiar one. You will have moments when you may feel that you don't need God— you can do it on our own. Robert's lesson is perhaps the most illuminating. You can get where you are going without God. But with God your journey can at times be easier and yield fewer pitfalls.

Scripture application: **Matthew 14:22-36**

Immediately Jesus made the disciples get into the boat and go on ahead of him to the other side, while he dismissed the crowd. After he had dismissed them, he went up on a mountainside by himself to pray. When evening came, he was there alone, but the boat was already a considerable distance from land, buffeted by the waves because the wind was against it. During the fourth watch of the night Jesus went out to them, walking on the lake. When the disciples saw him walking on the lake, they were terrified. "It's a ghost," they said, and cried out in fear. But Jesus immediately said to them: "Take courage! It is I. Don't be afraid." "Lord, if it's you," Peter replied, "tell me to come to you on the water." "Come," he said. Then Peter got down out of the boat, walked on the water and came toward Jesus. But when he saw the wind, he was afraid and, beginning to sink, cried out, "Lord, save me!" Immediately Jesus reached out his hand and caught him. "You of little faith," he said, "why did you doubt?" And when they climbed into the boat, the wind died down. Then those who were in the boat worshiped him, saying, "Truly you are the Son of God." When they had crossed over, they landed at Gennesaret. And when the men of that place recognized Jesus, they sent word to all the surrounding country. People brought all their sick to him and begged him to let the sick just touch the edge of his cloak, and all who touched him were healed.

Ephesians 2:8-10

For it is by grace you have been saved, through faith— and this not from yourselves, it is the gift of God— not by works, so that no one can boast. For we are God's workmanship, created in Christ Jesus to do good works, which God prepared in advance for us to do.

I'm just saying... | God can be trusted at all times. He can be trusted even when you can't trust yourself.

Are you, trusting God?

MY FAITH FILE ENTRY

_____

_____

_____

_____

_____

_____

_____

_____

_____

_____

_____

_____

_____

_____

_____

_____

_____

_____

_____

Choosing your **friends**

It has been said that we cannot pick our relatives but we can pick our friends. With that being the case, it is imperative that you choose wisely the people with whom you will associate for this next phase of your journey. Remember that in most relationships there are givers and takers. You will need to decide how much of each of these you want to have around you. Do you always want to be the one who gives the ride, lends the money, host the parties? A more important thing to consider is what do you get out of the relationship? Can the people surrounding you offer emotional support? Will they come to your aid in a pinch? When you no longer are on top of the world will these people still be your friends? I can tell you first hand. There will be times when life will deal you a terrible hand and all you want is for your friends to stand by you. You want your friends to have faith in who you are— to have your back. When this occurs you will really find out who your friends are. You will know the difference between associates and friends. Unfortunately, individuals that you thought were your friends, you will find were only passing acquaintances. But all is not lost, it is better to find out who your true friends are. Nothing weeds out friends from phonies more than a little controversy. Also, can these people speak in complete sentences? What can they give you intellectually? Is your friendship with these individuals a plus or a hindrance? Must you compromise your standards or can you be yourself? There is this saying that if you put a clean white shirt next to a dirty shirt, it is the clean white shirt which will become dirty. Never will the dirty shirt become clean. What am I saying to you? If your friends rub off on you make sure that what is rubbed onto you won't harm or hurt you. Undoubtedly, you have watched TV news when the announcer says.

"A crowd has gathered on the corner of Main and 1st. Young people have been placing stuffed animals in a makeshift memorial to the slain young man. Everyone said that John

was a good boy he was an honor student and not known to be a member of a gang. Through uncontrollable sobs, with shoulders shaking, Mary, his mother, cries "it was a case of mistaken identity. The shooter was looking for John's friend − Bill, the neighborhood drug dealer." John's association with Bill cost him his life − John's clean white shirt became dirty through his friendship with Bill."

Scripture application: **I Samuel 19:1-7**

Saul told his son Jonathan and all the attendants to kill David. But Jonathan was very fond of David and warned him, "My father Saul is looking for a chance to kill you. Be on your guard tomorrow morning; go into hiding and stay there. I will go out and stand with my father in the field where you are. I'll speak to him about you and will tell you what I find out." Jonathan spoke well of David to Saul his father and said to him, "Let not the king do wrong to his servant David; he has not wronged you, and what he has done has benefited you greatly. He took his life in his hands when he killed the Philistine. The Lord won a great victory for all Israel, and you saw it and were glad. Why then would you do wrong to an innocent man like David by killing him for no reason?" Saul listened to Jonathan and took this oath: "As surely as the Lord lives, David will not be put to death." So Jonathan called David and told him the whole conversation. He brought him to Saul, and David was with Saul as before.

The relationship between David and Jonathan the son of King Saul depicts a true friendship. Both individuals brought something to the table, both offered support and genuine friendship. The friendship sustained through what could have been a contentious situation. Even when David, was no longer favored by King Saul, no longer at the top of his game, no longer the top dog, Jonathan's friendship remained true, and he helped him escape plots to end David's life.

I'm just saying...

Choose your friends wisely. Has your shirt been dirtied or does it remain clean?

Is Jesus your friend?

MY FAITH FILE ENTRY

_____

_____

_____

_____

_____

_____

_____

_____

_____

_____

_____

_____

_____

_____

_____

_____

_____

_____

_____

_____

It is not what you're called,
it's what you answer to

I know that scripture mentions that God hates a proud look and pride falls before the man, but this lesson has nothing to do with being vain. There are moments in life, when "the haters" will try their best to put you down, to more or less kill your ambitions in life by making you feel inadequate. When my kids were teenagers, like most teens, they cared deeply about their outward appearance. They only wanted to wear designer clothes, the latest fashions etc. If they did not have the latest pair of Jordan gym shoes, Polo brand shirt, their life would fall apart or so they thought. What they wanted was acceptance into the "in crowd" to be cool and together. They like many, mistakenly believed that who you were on the inside was dependent on what you looked like on the outside. Well one day my youngest daughter came home very upset. She found herself the target of the local bully's teasing. It so happened, that Camille was singled out by the bully as being stuck up and conceited because she did not speak in slang, but spoke correct English and used proper grammar. She dressed well and took pride in her appearance.

This bully called Camille almost everything but a child of God. Camille did not know how to respond. I took this opportunity to tell her about being "convinced." I began explaining to my daughter her family history, beginning with her great, great, great, great grandmother Chaney Richie, a Virginia slave. The history lesson concluded with her great uncle Boston and grandfather Oscar Richie, owners of the family trucking business, which bears our name, Boston Richie Trucking. I told her that some kids lash out at those who dared to think for themselves. Self-assured individuals were at times called names and picked on. A bully does not have a sense of who he or she is and they themselves were the ones who felt inadequate.

I told her that once people know that she is a Richie she might be called conceited and should come to expect it. She is also to take the time to educate her antagonizer. The Encarta Dictionary's definition of conceited is: *"too proud, having or showing an excessively high opinion of your own qualities or abilities."* I told her that she should not fret, because we as Richies were not now nor ever been conceited. Being conceited is when you "think" you are all that and a bag of chips, but as Richies we were "convinced" that we were all that and a bag of chips. I explained to her that as Richies we were somebody, we mattered, we were important.

Now here is the lesson, it is not because of our last name, it is because we are children of the Most High God. **Psalm 134:14** explains that we are fearfully and wonderfully made, a peculiar people of royal priesthood. Why? because we have been adopted into the family of Christ, and if God my father is rich in houses and land, and has given all power and authority to his son Jesus Christ, then who are we to walk around being embarrassed as to who we are.

I told her the world may call you a lot of things, but always remember it is not what you are called it is what you answer to. Instead of being conceited, which is really not being sure of who you are, we are to be convinced who we are. If we are convinced it does not matter what a bully calls you. A bully cannot make you anything that you are not.

Scripture application: **Psalm 134:14**

Explains that we are fearfully and wonderfully made, a peculiar people of royal priesthood.

I'm just saying...

Don't let the world define you!

Are you convinced?

MY FAITH FILE ENTRY

_____

_____

_____

_____

_____

_____

_____

_____

_____

_____

_____

_____

_____

_____

_____

_____

_____

Don't give **up!**

So often, young people as well as adults have a tendency to give up when things get tough or the outlook is bleak and uncertain. In the summer of 2010, my brother Wayne, mother Gladys, and I along with my mother's brother Donald and sister Betty were returning to Springfield after having attended a funeral of a family member in Aberdeen, Mississippi.

We were about 20 to 30 miles south of St. Louis, Missouri when we could see a storm forming ahead in the distance. The further along we traveled the blacker the sky became. Jagged streaks of lightning crisscrossed in the sky and quickly disappeared only to be followed by loud claps of thunder. Bam, crack and all of the sudden, the winds picked up. Driving was beginning to become difficult. It wasn't too long before we could hear and feel the thunder and lightning.

Someone, from the rear of the van asked the question, "do you think we will drive into the storm?" My reply, "all we can do is, see where this road takes us." We crept ever so close to the storm. We could see in the midst of the turbulent black clouds a small swatch of grey. The road, (I-55 North) lead us straight to the grey in the sky. Without warning the skies opened and the rain came pouring down on us. We looked to the right and to the left and realized that we were on the periphery of the most violent part of the storm. We were in the storm, but not the worst part of it.

The car in front of us, pulled over to the side of the road. "So what you going to do," I heard my brother ask, "pull over or forge ahead." I slowed the speed of the van, gripped the wheel, focused and drove ahead. The road twisted and turned in the Missouri hills. Just as suddenly as the clouds had earlier gathered to unleash a torrential downpour, the clouds retreated. The rain stopped. The sun claimed victory and once again reigned supreme in the sky.

We looked behind us wondering about the car that pulled over— to us the driver had more or less given up. From where we could see, this car was stuck on the side of the road still in the middle of the storm.

The lesson I share with you is don't give up. Life at times will produce ominous clouds in the form of disappointments, failures, loneliness and at times mistreatment by others. These storms may appear suddenly without warning.

If you just slow down, gather yourself, focus and hold fast to your belief in God, he will bring you through whatever storm your particular road in life carries you.

It is true that you might find yourself in some sort of storm, however if you look around without panicking you will find things are not as bad as they could be. You will discover that you are in the grey sitting on the periphery of what could be worse, and for that you ought to thank God.

The key is not to give up— keep moving forward. If not, you might find that you are stuck on the side of the road, forever in a storm. A storm, which should have only lasted for you a short while, but because you gave up, the storm, keeps on raging.

Scripture application: **Luke 8:22-25**

Jesus Calms the Storm

One day Jesus said to his disciples, "Let's go over to the other side of the lake." So they got into a boat and set out. As they sailed, he fell asleep. A squall came down on the lake, so that the boat was being swamped, and they were in great danger. The disciples went and woke him, saying, "Master, Master, we're going to drown!" He got up and rebuked the wind and the raging waters; the storm subsided, and all was calm. "Where is your faith?" he asked his disciples. In fear and amazement they asked one another, "Who is this? He commands even the winds and the water, and they obey him."

I'm just saying...

In life we will always face adversity but it's what you do in those adverse times that matters.

Are you stuck on the side of the road?

MY FAITH FILE ENTRY

_____

_____

_____

_____

_____

_____

_____

_____

_____

_____

_____

_____

_____

_____

_____

_____

_____

_____

_____

Now and **later**

Esau returning from a hunt was starving, famished to the point of death or so he thought. He came to his brother and demanded to be fed. His brother, the more shrewd of the two saw an opportunity. He sees his brother in a weakened and vulnerable state and he convinces his brother to trade his birthright for a bowl of soup or stew. But more significant— Esau satisfied a now moment of perceived urgency and squandered the blessing which was to come later.

How could he allow this to happen? By all accounts he was a man of nature, he knew how to hunt, and fish. He knew what was edible in the wilderness and what was not. He satisfied the now moment of hunger because he devalued his birthright. I don't know if he did this because he thought the later was so far away, that he did not have to worry about his birthright. You know dad had okay health; he was going to around for awhile. What do I care about this birthright? It can't do me any good right now. But his brother Jacob, the shrewd one, he knew the value of the birthright. Esau allowed himself, to be placed in a vulnerable position or situation.

What could Esau have done differently even before he saw his brother? He could have been better prepared for the hunt. After all, he was the hunter. He could have taken an adequate supply of water and something to eat. He could have returned prior to the point of being starved. To put it succinctly, he could have planned. But since he did not he was forced to satisfy a now moment and forfeit his later blessing.

I have always told my children "think past your arm." Meaning the choices you make in the immediate will affect you later. You and a group of friends are at the mall— one say's let's take or steal something. You have a choice— go ahead and steal now and face the later consequences of momma's belt, and a criminal record. A record will stay with you for a lifetime. Or you can not steal and continue to enjoy the trust of your parents, and no criminal record.

How can you plan? By choosing your friends wisely, setting the record straight before you hook up. You have a choice, not study for a test now and face the good possibility of failing the test later. Or you can study now and stand a good chance of passing the test later. Freshmen and sophomores need to know that how they perform at this grade level will determine their grade point average and class rank by the time they are juniors and seniors. Plan now or suffer the consequences later. How is this important? Scholarships are given out according to grade point and class rank. Admission to college is based on grade point and class rank.

Plan now or suffer consequences later. Sex— girls— plan now. Don't allow yourselves to be placed in a weakened and vulnerable position or predicament. You most assuredly know of girls that failed to plan and found themselves in a weakened vulnerable position and had an outcome not to their liking nine months later. Boys— the same for you. It is fun now but later as Kanye West says "18 years, 18 years, now she's got your for 18 years."

Relationships— there is a saying "don't burn your bridges." You know you get into an argument or disagreement with someone maybe even a friend. Before you know it, you say something in the heat of the now. You have satisfied your now moment of anger but what about the later. Do you really think that your paths won't cross again? Do you really think that you won't need that person again? Your only hope is that this person is more spiritual than you are, and he or she is able to forgive. Life is about choices and making the right choices.

Esau gave up something that would have blessed him the rest of his life, all for the immediate satisfaction of the now.

Scripture application: **Genesis 25:19-34**

This is the account of Abraham's son Isaac. Abraham became the father of Isaac, and Isaac was forty years old when he married Rebekah daughter of Bethuel the Aramean from Paddan Aram and sister of Laban the Aramean. Isaac prayed to the Lord on behalf of his wife, because she was barren. The Lord answered his prayer, and his wife Rebekah became pregnant. The babies jostled each other within her, and she said, "Why is this happening to me?" So she went to inquire of the Lord. The Lord said to her, "Two nations are in your womb, and two peoples from within you will be separated; one people will be stronger than the other, and the older will serve the younger."

When the time came for her to give birth, there were twin boys in her womb. The first to come out was red, and his whole body was like a hairy garment; so they named him Esau. After this, his brother came out, with his hand grasping Esau's heel; so he was named Jacob.? Isaac was sixty years old when Rebekah gave birth to them. The boys grew up, and Esau became a skillful hunter, a man of the open country, while Jacob was a quiet man, staying among the tents. Isaac, who had a taste for wild game, loved Esau, but Rebekah loved Jacob. Once when Jacob was cooking some stew, Esau came in from the open country, famished. He said to Jacob, "Quick, let me have some of that red stew! I'm famished!" Jacob replied, "First sell me your birthright." "Look, I am about to die," Esau said. "What good is the birthright to me?" But Jacob said, "Swear to me first." So he swore an oath to him, selling his birthright to Jacob. Then Jacob gave Esau some bread and some lentil stew. He ate and drank, and then got up and left.

So Esau despised his birthright.

I'm just saying... | Satisfying the now in your life may jeopardize your Later.

Are you making the right choices?

MY FAITH FILE ENTRY

_____

_____

_____

_____

_____

_____

_____

_____

_____

_____

_____

_____

_____

_____

_____

_____

_____

Guard your **dreams**

Do not share your 8 x 10 dreams with someone who can only think in a 4 x 6 frame. Why? Because that person will not be able to think as deep or as broad as you. That person will be forced to cut away at your dreams and even trample on them in order for your dreams to fit in their limited scope of thinking.

Have you ever looked for encouragement from a friend about something you really wanted to do, only to be shot down? Perhaps it was your desire to go to a certain four year university, only to be told trade school or the military better fits you. Perhaps you wanted to start your own business only to be told that "they" don't see it in your future.

Your dreams and goals are yours— Jesus Christ will enhance you, grow you, encourage you not stifle or inhibit your potential.

Scripture application: **Genesis 37:1-11**

Jacob lived in the land where his father had stayed, the land of Canaan.

This is the account of Jacob.

Joseph, a young man of seventeen, was tending the flocks with his brothers, the sons of Bilhah and the sons of Zilpah, his father's wives, and he brought their father a bad report about them.

Now Israel loved Joseph more than any of his other sons, because he had been born to him in his old age; and he made a richly ornamented robe for him. When his brothers saw that their father loved him more than any of them, they hated him and could not speak a kind word to him.

Joseph had a dream, and when he told it to his brothers, they hated him all the more. He said to them, "Listen to this dream I had: We were binding sheaves of grain out in the field when suddenly my sheaf rose and stood upright, while your sheaves gathered around mine and bowed down to it."

His brothers said to him, "Do you intend to reign over us? Will you actually rule us?" And they hated him all the more because of his dream and what he had said.

Then he had another dream, and he told it to his brothers. "Listen," he said, "I had another dream, and this time the sun and moon and eleven stars were bowing down to me."

When he told his father as well as his brothers, his father rebuked him and said, "What is this dream you had? Will your mother and I and your brothers actually come and bow down to the ground before you?" His brothers were jealous of him, but his father kept the matter in mind.

I'm just saying...

It is okay to dream and to share your dreams but be careful of your circle of friends.

Are you sharing your life's ambitions and desires with Christ?

MY FAITH FILE ENTRY

_____

_____

_____

_____

_____

_____

_____

_____

_____

_____

_____

_____

_____

_____

_____

_____

_____

Go and possess **the land**

"See, I have given you this land. Go in and take possession of the land that the LORD swore he would give to your fathers— to Abraham, Isaac and Jacob— and to their descendants after them."

— Deuteronomy 1:8 NIV

The Israelites were at the end of their 40 years of wandering in the dessert. They were about to walk into God's promise. 12 men were selected to go into the promise land to search it out. The 12 came back and reported seeing huge clusters of grapes. 10 of the 12 men told the Israelites that the land was flowing with milk and honey. Along with the favorable report came the disturbing news that on the land lived giants. In their eyes the ten viewed themselves and grasshoppers and said they would never be able to defeat those giants. How could they take over the land?

Who told the ten that they were like grasshoppers and could not defeat the giants?

The ten lacked faith in God. This same God delivered their ancestors from the land of the Pharaoh. God sustained them for 40 years in the wilderness. But with all God had done for them, the ten spies lacked faith. They looked at the natural circumstances and saw that the inhabitants of the land were big. Their view of themselves lacked self esteem. They viewed themselves as inferior and believed that there was no humanly way to defeat the giants. The land could never belong to them.

Thank God for Joshua and Caleb (the other two spies). Their report back to the Israelites acknowledged the giants but also acknowledged the God they served. Yes, the giants lived in the land but God promised the land to them. "It's ours we must go and possess it." Caleb and Joshua had faith in a God who had saved them before. Caleb and Joshua looked into their faith files. Caleb and Joshua were there when God parted the Red Sea to let Moses and the Israelites cross over a dry sea bed. Caleb and Joshua were there when manna rained from heaven.

Caleb and Joshua had faith. You know what? Those with no faith never possessed the land.

Because, of their faith in God, Joshua and Caleb were able to go and possess the land.

Some of you have aspirations of going to college. God has made a way.

Some of you have dreams of starting your own businesses. God has opened the door.

For some of you there are employment opportunities in your future. God has put you in contact with the right people to make this happen.

Some of you prayed for a spouse, and God has shown him or her to you.

But before your dreams are realized, mountains appear, naysayers cry out, and bad news comes.

How will you view your circumstances: grasshoppers versus giants? What do you believe?

I'm just saying...

In life you will be faced with circumstances and events that you might feel are unbeatable. The mountains which you must climb will seem like they are insurmountable. The medical report from the doctor will seem devastating.

But, God has promised you that he will never leave you nor forsake you.

Isaiah states that with God no weapon formed against you will prosper.

Jeremiah tells us that God has plans for your life, not to harm you but to prosper you, to give you a hope and a future.

If God promised it, it is yours. What God has for you, is for you.

Giant or grasshopper?

Go and possess the land!

MY FAITH FILE ENTRY

_____

_____

_____

_____

_____

_____

_____

_____

_____

_____

_____

_____

_____

_____

_____

_____

_____

_____

Psalm 37:1-11; 34-40

A Psalm of David.

Do not fret because of evil men or be envious of those who do wrong; for like the grass they will soon wither, like green plants they will soon die away. Trust in the Lord and do good; dwell in the land and enjoy safe pasture. Delight yourself in the Lord and he will give you the desires of your heart. Commit your way to the Lord; trust in him and he will do this: He will make your righteousness shine like the dawn, the justice of your cause like the noonday sun. Be still before the Lord and wait patiently for him; do not fret when men succeed in their ways, when they carry out their wicked schemes. Refrain from anger and turn from wrath; do not fret—it leads only to evil. For evil men will be cut off, but those who hope in the Lord will inherit the land. A little while, and the wicked will be no more; though you look for them, they will not be found. But the meek will inherit the land and enjoy great peace.

Psalm 37:34-40

Wait for the Lord and keep his way. He will exalt you to inherit the land; when the wicked are cut off, you will see it. I have seen a wicked and ruthless man flourishing like a green tree in its native soil, but he soon passed away and was no more; though I looked for him, he could not be found. Consider the blameless, observe the upright; there is a future for the man of peace. But all sinners will be destroyed; the future of the wicked will be cut off. The salvation of the righteous comes from the Lord; he is their stronghold in time of trouble. The Lord helps them and delivers them; he delivers them from the wicked and saves them, because they take refuge in him.